tumble

tumble

Joanna Preston

OTAGO UNIVERSITY PRESS
Te Whare Tā o Te Wānanga o Ōtākou

In memory of my teachers:

Mary Harris (1906–2011)
Grant Andrews (1960–2013)
and Helen Bascand (1929–2015)

Contents

All tribal myths are true, for a given value of 'true'.
– *Terry Pratchett*

Female, nude

The things we prize. Innocence,
the sleeping fire that speaks

through the long white flower
of her spine, the curve

of her hips the rim of a slow
turning wheel

on which to break a man.

i.

Lucifer in Las Vegas

tortoise: from the Greek tartaroukhos: *'of the underworld'*

i. The fall

As I fell, I burned
through shame and grief
and disbelief and love –
words that trail
like broken wings.
Only rage was left –
its silken tongue, its
crystal shell. I fell
through night and time
into the morning
of this world, and kept
on falling.
Once, I lived
by passion's flame,
but I learned

cold blood
is better.

ii. Shell

It's been six thousand years,
give or take. This shape's as good
as any other. I am fortress,
island, rock – a treasure chest

with a living lock no thief
can pick. I walk in armour,
plastron thicker than a tank.

The only mark of then
is a reflex twitch, a flinch,
a body thing I still can't shake
beneath the fear of wings.

When I heard what happened
to Aeschylus, I laughed so hard
I nearly split my shell. Well,
I see He hasn't lost His sense
of humour.

iii. Sand

Once, all this was sand. Sand and cactus,
sand and yuccas, sand and black brush,
gila monsters, sand and sand. Hell
of a place to land in,

                a dried-out basin
in the mountains. Not a blade
of grass to graze on, not a flower
without thorns.

            I listened
to the blood-song of the desert

and dug down.

iv. Vegas

I built this kingdom for myself
from memories.

        The dry-bones chatter
of dice from a rattler's tail, and the girls
pink and gold like gaudy birds.

The card shoe started out an empty
tortoise shell (I bear no rivals),

baize-covered tables for the cropped
green fuzz that gave this town its name.
And the one-armed bandits – sheer genius,
like teaching cows to milk themselves.

The gambling chips began as skutes, then clay,
then plastic.
             Now I use men's souls.
Why not? They're plentiful and light, and have
no other value but my mark.

We do it all – the wedding, the ensuing divorce,
the post-loss suicide. If you want it,
you can get it.

At a price.

v. Lucifer

In the desert, the night sky
was endless. In the desert
the night sky was achingly near

but now it feels empty.
Abandoned. Mere clouds of dust
condensed into stars and space.
I stopped searching
its blank face for signs
of forgiveness aeons ago.

       Look down.
From the high-stakes room
the glitter of money
puts starshine to shame.
Look down. All the people
who flock to my shepherds, who pray
at my temples …

       Look down.
I hurl a handful
of orange chips into the air –
watch the sheep scrabble
and crawl at my feet.

       At night, look down
from space and Vegas is
the brightest thing on this world.

Look down, damn you, and see.

Classical Gas

How does the sky pick its colour? The summer
Dad bought his guitar, the colour lifted
from three hydrangeas, growing where Grandma
emptied the chamber pot each morning.

Cicadas strumming in the crepe myrtle,
their shed skins like twists of cellophane
still clinging to the bark. The summer
I came down hard on the edge
of the verandah, gouged a perfect
plectrum of bone from my shin.

I didn't fall – I flew. The hydrangeas
reached out and caught me, held me
in the fretwork of their flowers.
It was the silky oak that bled.
It was a satin bird that shrieked.
The verandah lay silent, listening
to Dad pluck his way through the heat.

Chronicle of the year 793

This year, half gone, has worn heavy.
A sickness plagued the cattle,
and many were lost. A blight
has afflicted the crops –
the ears of grain grow sticky and dark
and will not ripen.

What we have to share, we give,
but so many are hungry.
When the king left, Father Higbald
stripped the hangings and plate
from his room, sent the sacristan
to sell what he could and buy bread
for the weakest, for the children.

And still the portents come.
Dragons in flight, great flashes
of fire from a cloudless sky.
The miller's son ran wild – tore
at the skin of his chest and arms
until it hung in bloodied ribbons.
He saw visions. Demon faces
leered from the walls
he said. A day later he died.

Stranger still, at vespers three nights ago
a great flock of birds blackened the sky.
People cried out, or fled, or clung
to the altar cloths.

So many birds! Yet afterwards
not one feather was found
to name them.

And now again! Strange,
how their wingbeats sound
like oars.

A bird in the hand

i.
The tale told afterwards
was of his chastity –

how he'd forced a young woman
into a bed

of nettles

the fire without
to quench the fire within

to douse her ardour
he said.

ii.
Merula, the dark girl with golden eyes
who came to his hand
like a bird

her lips against his lips
a sacrament

how she taught him to read
the braille scripture
of body
and body

her fingers as light as fimbria,
her feet
bare and barely leaving a mark

except in him.

iii.
She led him
into the underworld –
this he knew
as he knew her.

She opened for him
the flesh

of a pomegranate,
told him to sip, taste,
take.

He fell with the world
into winter.

iv.
And afterwards
was the tale of the blackbird
who'd built a nest
in his outstretched palm –

once more
and he might believe it,
forget

dark hair tangling
with his own,
the blood in his ears
like the beating of wings

his broken sky
the blue
of eggshell.

The elephant in the parlour

The piano did not expect this, these
furtive stirrings, like a mouse, nesting deep
in its cabinet, turning and turning
against the trembling soundboard.
A daughter of the house – the piano remembers
about daughters – anointed its keys with salt water
and the satin benediction of her cheek.
The piano presses gently back
into the fingertips that flutter across ivory,
fills the singing length of every note
with the timbre of its longing. So patient,
it will wait in the gloom of the house
settling around it, a temple giving way
to the coming of the forest. It knows
in its iron bones, ebony and leafmould,
the shadow under vines damping down
its velvet hammers, the long-forgotten key
of solitude broken off in its lock.

Woman in the water

You came unlooked-for,
and unlocked their faces. Rival.
Intruder. A flaxen stranger
from my family's past –
I fiercely wished you back there.

But you stayed. Borrowed
my mother's swimsuit
and they sent me to show you the way
to the swimming hole,

      dark, and
      so deep
where the current
carves into the bend.

The only sounds made
were whispers – your fingers
unplaiting your rope of hair,
the rocks' angry tongues to my feet.

      Half lost,

half won, I asked did you want me
to stay, to – No. *Thank you.*
      You turned away

and dived in, swam out, hair trailing
across the surface, a gleaming arc,

light through the crack of a doorway
to one trapped inside, in the dark.

Silks

She straddled the ridge-cap. Against her legs
the day's warmth, trapped in the roof tiles, felt
comforting, almost alive. Nearby, someone
was burning leaves – a sweet smell, like toffee.
Across the fences, the trees were in autumn's silks –
russet and gold, chestnut and bay. She gripped lightly
with her knees, as she'd been taught. She didn't want
wings. She wanted to fly on the thunder of hooves,
feel muscles surging beneath her. The word
in her head, matching stride – *free-ee-dom,*
free-ee-dom, free-ee-dom – as she bent low
over the withers, pressing her cheek
against the finial's neck, her own hair
a mane, streaming wild in the wind.

The dollhouse

Through the window, with its wimple of lace
into a room where no clock ever strikes,
no book ever rustles its pages. The painting
on the wall is mathematically straight,
and the two armchairs face each other
slant, like lawyers.
                          Further in, and a girl
in frilled socks, her hair in neat plaits
is dressing her dolls before breakfast.
Here is the mother: here is her apron.
Here is the father: here are his trousers,
painted on. Here is his shirt, freshly pressed.
Here is his briefcase, his necktie, his car keys.
Here are the mother's blood-red stilettos.
Here is the mother's short skirt.
                          And here
is the kitchen table, the three chairs,
three plates. Here are the three spoons
that catch the light, and the two adults
who will not catch each other's eyes, no matter
how their daughter contorts them.

Atalanta

She is running,
leaves underfoot, great drifts
as though she were running
through the soft husks of summer.

She is spreading the wings
of her lungs, running
away from them, businessmen
queued at the traffic lights
thinking of home.

In dreams it feels like this –
effortless. Stride and breath flowing
like sunlight through half-bare trees.

At the end of the path she will stop,
catch her breath, her day
stealing back with the flush
on her face.

But for now she is running. The tingle
of sweat meeting cold air,
the exhilaration,

as though she could outrun her life.

The cold, darkening

Coming in to roost
the flocks of starlings
dip and sweep
trailing filaments of dusk

and then settle in
to the weft of trees,
anchoring night
with their feet.

The toymaker's daughter

I remember a butterfly, asleep on the frame
of the cobbler's door, across the alley.
The summer the fortune-teller came, warning
of broken vows and bones. My father
cursed, turned the dogs on him.
I fled to the forest by dawn.

The trees have song beyond hearing,
and it rises in me.
Through every storm that followed
my skin drummed with their call.
My mother's tears
were rain on parched leaves.
I hung through winter, flesh falling.

I remember the candle she lit
in the window, fat as the moon,
smelling of pine. How the wick danced
with its burden of flame. How her hands shook
when he took to me. When I see her now,
through bare branches, her grief
is an artist's fancy.

The trees have taught me to weather,
to bend and sway and drive my roots deep.
Tell him I've buried his axe
in a mountain, his knives
one by one in the wind. Tell him
the trees remember his face.
Tell my mother nothing.

Portrait of Great-Aunt Lavinia as a bathysphere

So reinforced – her waist, the bounty
of her chest, her coral reef of painted hair –

you'd swear she'd walk away unharmed
from being struck by lightning, by
a trolley-car, by a sudden fancy

to walk down to the quay, and keep on walking

past the shops – shuttered now, and sleeping – past
the window where they sell the ferry tickets,

past the nīkau, holding up and out their palms
in meditation or supplication,

past the bollards, counting off the waves
along the pier, and on and off the end

into the water.

And now she finds that water

is her element. Bubbles are a shoal
of fish that shimmer round her, and she

is open-mouthed with love.

She sinks deeper, her skirts a plume
of jellyfish, her shoes a pair of cuttlefish,
unlacing and retreating in a puff of coloured ink.

Her hair uncoils slowly from its braids,
trailing languorous above her, like her fingers,

a farewell to the air-soaked world above,

and I know that she crossed gladly, slipped
into the boundless kingdom of the ocean,

leaving nothing but her name, a story
touched with brine.

Leaving

I thought I heard him calling as I crossed
the town boundary, out past the saleyards,

years ago. But the dusk was in my eyes
and I would not turn back, never again

choke on the dust of that place. Escape
was a highway driven through those days.

I raised a cathedral, and locked its doors.
Bound that ambush, memory,

and branded it slave. But still I hear
sometimes, in the rattle of cattle trucks,

his voice, or mine. And I forget
how to sleep. A voice shouting, sounds

as much as words. *Come back, please!* perhaps.
Or maybe – *Run.*

ii.

Lijessenthoek

> the fields of Flanders –
> rich red
> of the cemetery gates

There. Red brick and white stone; an archway anything but
triumphal. We wheeled our hired bicycles through the gate-
building, blinking at the transition from light to shadow to
light again as we stepped out into the garden. And garden
it was. Rows of lilies, ranged in front of the crosses that
marked the Canadian graves. The New Zealand graves. The
South African graves. But not cut flowers – every grave had
a flowering plant growing by the headstone, watered and
weeded and tended. A garden! How must it feel, to be a
gardener here?

> a late baptism –
> thirty-four christened
> 'known unto God'

We found his grave. Row 21D. 4564 Corporal Stanley
Coombes, 45th Battalion Australian Infantry, died 12th
October 1917. I took photographs to send home, the first of
our family to visit this place since he died. His full name, place
of birth, the names of his parents and his home, written in a
ledger almost too heavy for me to lift.

He was twenty-four when he was wounded and sent back
home, only to be told that he would die of tuberculosis, likely
soon. Twenty-four when he chose to return to the front.
Twenty-four when he was wounded at the third battle of

Ypres – the Battle of Passchendaele – to die of his injuries a
few days later in a casualty clearing station in the village of
Lijessenthoek.

> family photos –
> they say I have his
> eyebrows

There were hop bines growing in a field on the other side of
the cemetery. Pale green, twisting up their wires and into the
sky. Fitting somehow, that beside ten thousand dead they plant
and harvest each year a herb of bitterness, and comfort.

> suddenly understanding
> why there are no
> old trees

I've read his diaries. Stained and smudged, they were sent
home to my great-great-grandmother. He wrote quietly about
fear, and mud, and missing the sound of the currawongs in
the evenings. And how, one day like any other, a line of them
were trudging across the duckboards when a sniper took out
the man behind him. He said he felt the grip of the other man's
hand tighten briefly, and then let go.

The disembodied woman

It's the delicate feedback-loop of sensation
from joint and muscle and the pale sheath
of your own skin that tells you
you have a body, a physical location.
Tonight, all the gods are at a party –

I was invited, but what would I wear?
A body the world knows better than me?
It started simply – I was my mother's
mistake. I left my name, dyed my hair.
Did I ever feel? I can't remember.

I lose my hands. Break concentration
and they're not where I expect them to be.
Stupid. It takes all my skill to hold onto
a knife, say, and a conversation.
Nerveless fingers, white with pressure.

I remember I swayed, unsteady on my feet
and they whistled and cheered. So I filed
half an inch off every left heel. They
loved me. When I couldn't breathe
they said I sounded sexy.

A body, blind and deaf to itself,
artifice making up what nature lacks.
I know I belong to the audience.
I've never belonged to anything else. They
made me their mirror. The crumpled cover

of every other magazine. Sometimes
I can't even imagine that other girl.
But tracing the curve of these lips
I almost remember when they were mine
and real. In Peter's Spyder, driving like hell

with the top down. Wind rushing
against my arms and face to tell me, yes
I *have* two arms, a face. Not a ghost
lost in some painted, posed machine,
too statuesque, too consciously maintained.

I married for love once. It didn't last.
Now I am numb. Heavy-lidded. Grateful.
Half listening for footsteps. Footlights. No, headlines.
Headlights sweep across the room, make the water glass
on its side twinkle, twinkle. I can almost reach them.

Lineage

Of necessity, and in accordance
with our custom, her mother's sisters
are singing her a husband.

The way of it was written
in an ancient book, or possibly
graven in tablets of iron, or
if not in iron, then painted
in ochre upon cave walls.

The voices rise to strike
against the flintlock stars –
they catch, flare,
flutter and fall to earth
like ash, dug into soil to sweeten it.

A click, as she ungirdles her arms,
and he is there. A sigh
as he kneels to kiss
the pages of her feet.

Only then will it be safe
to unlock the doors of the cavity
where he keeps his heart

– an intricate device,
of parchment and copper wires –
and set it ticking.

Criccieth

I walked the length of the beach
into the wind off Tremadog Bay.
Shingle, not sand under my feet.
Ropes of kelp wrenched free
in the storm last night
marked the limit of the tide.
By the mouth of the Dwyfor
the bleached hide and scattered bones
of a long-dead sheep
warned against straying.

I found a stone – pupil-black, and as smooth
as an ancient gannet's egg.
It fitted into my palm, and filled my hand
as your hand did.

Wintering over

Here, true winter comes stalking across the moor,
bristling with Siberia. We retreat to the safety of our
double-glazed burrows, spend winter severed from
the world, gnawing through our stores of fat and
familial tolerance. Waiting out the winter, until the
nights too begin to shrink, and the sun makes a wobbly
reappearance over slate roofs. Then we'll emerge,
blinking in light become unfamiliar – every winter is
the first winter, every spring is the first spring. Survey
our neighbours, reckon the survivors.

> unbroken snow –
> the shadow of a stone wall
> lengthening

The salmon

Already a bone-deep rumble
becomes a roar too loud
too low not
to be disaster

its stippled belly swollen
with four hundred strangers,
it hangs in the current of night
above my bed
                      they
are oblivious.

Darkness like water
darkness thick and corporeal
the moor opens in front of them,
hillsides aching to reclaim their metals.

Stewardesses in their regimentals
flicker along the cabin
to take their seats for landing.

They think they're going home.

Wingtips glisten green and red,
safe, and *caution*
warning
danger

       midwife of fiery endings.

Rumble becomes roar becomes the howl
of air torn apart by landing-gear,
salmo salar; salmon, the leaper
fighting the spate of gravity

a surge, and it passes above me,
and onward and up and a flick of its tail
and up

at the rim

of the valley

Lost

The day after our second anniversary
the mountains
tried to take you from me.

A stranger at the door
speaking the name that I
still thought of
as your mother's. The colour
drained out of my clothes
                              until
they were as white
as an avalanche.

.

A woman with my face, adrift
in a room filled with the quiet voice
of snow.

.

The stone weight of cold
punched the windows in
and swept you off the road –

our life
streaming past with a roar that I
was drowning in and nothing any
where for me to cling
to

and then silence.

                    .

        I dreamed you *safe*.
        I dreamed you *free* and *home again*.
        I waited in the wreckage
        until the moon shone in my eyes
        like headlights

                    .

and they found you.
Fallen stars, like shards of glass,
scattered through your hair.

Census at Bethlehem

after Bruegel

She has become a sounding bell,
leaden, heavy-laden,
gathering the miles into a rope,
knots of aching anchored
to her spine.
The journey has rung through her,
and now it ends, in muteness,
in the sleepfulness of snow.

But not purity – the white is everywhere
churned to mire and muck
by counted feet, even
the sky a freezing burden.
Her cloak is gathered only
at her throat, like a secret
held under her tongue.

And the sense
of movement, even still,
the moment bearing her along.

The man she calls husband, his
back to her, his anger
and its ash. Her sin,
her single *yes* – she bloomed with it,
she drank the risen sun.

The skeletons of carts, wheel and shaft,
the ruined castle and the frozen lake.
She knows. Her part is nearly over,
and no matter what she chose, all
that she will know now
is this cold.

In camera

I remember his hands, reaching for me.
A foundling, a beggar, a box of tricks,
an unroofed chamber, an empty camera.
He filled me with light, a stippled language
of our own devising, of shadow and luminance,
coaxing immortality from silver plate
and mercury vapour. He is gone,
but she and I remain.

When first she came to pose for him,
he patrolled the space between
with words. She'd ask
if her pose was correct, if
she'd held herself still enough.
He would toss the answer
over his shoulder, embroidered
just to confound her.
But when she left, I could feel
the tremors she set in him.
How she marred his purpose. The harm.

Days became weeks, and yet
he could not find a way to capture her.
Night after night the sheets
were a tangle of weeds, sleep
a dark, dank hole, that he must climb
down, again and again.

Each morning he'd polish the metal plate,
his face a ghost, latent in its sheen.
And she would come, and he
would talk, would rant, his moods
a fairy-tale thicket sprung up between them.
How patiently she gathered each blossom,
every thorn, into a corsage abloom on her shoulder.
Sure as ripe fruit begets wasps. As longing
begets sin. So he gave in.

None of us leaves anything but traces:
a narrow bunk for sleeping, a camera
with a broken lens, a shabby velvet case
and a daguerreotype so real-looking you'd swear
you saw her fingers move – a woman
in a flowered chiffon dress, the tarnished
umbra of her face.

Margaret of Finchley

A nacreous lustre, softened
light around a core
of iron. Wave upon wave
above a twinset hauberk
and pearls. This
we knew, the curtain
twitched aside. A woman,
doing women's work –
the dirty stuff, the rough
– make clean, make right,
make do. She will not turn
to comfort you,
resolute in the set
of her shoulders. Mark
the scar, the brand,
the iron spine. This
is no game. Her embrace
does not bear thinking of –
it will crush you.
Darling.

Galanthus in rain

Soft rain bends the necks of winter flowers –
penitents in white veils and green blouses,
meek beneath the copper beech that towers
like a magistrate. And all my powers
of persuasion cannot alter how this
grim gallows-verdict falls: you are now hers.
Shapeless as salt water, thirty hours
since you left. Who knew we were such cowards?
– good wine set aside until it sours.
The house fills with rain. And I allow this.

Fault

A mistake. An error of judgement. A penalty
brought against a quiet city. Stroll
through the park, lunchtime almost over.
A defect, a small disappointment. A summer day
laden with clouds, grey light that softens the walls,
the stone and brick, the glass. Less
than expected. Someone to blame. A sparrow
rests lightly on the hand of a statue. A weakness
in the system, communications break down.
A telephone rings into silence. A refusal. Dispraise, dis-
continuity, lateral displacement. A woman
leaves a café, checks both ways, crosses the street.
An unthought response. A vice. Students repeating
the phrases – *good morning, good evening, good-
bye*. It is nine o'clock, it is ten to eleven. The time
is twelve fifty-one.

The Ministry of Sorrow

Build it of stone, of brick, of twisted
metal. Build it of shattering masonry.
Build it of glass. Build it of cards
of condolence. Build it of tears. Build it
of lives, of lies, of lying alone
with the stone of absence filling your belly.

Build it of stars. Build it of asphalt. Build it of shoes
by the bed. Build it of wounds. Build it
of sutures. Build it of sirens and smoke alarms,
build it of false alarms, build it of falling
and bruising and broken bones.
Build it of unanswered telephone calls
at four a.m., and the hours torn open till dawn.

Build it of sleeplessness. Build it of anxiousness.
Build it of thankfulness. Build it of guilt,
the gilded lobby and marble stares. Build it
of doctors and firemen and mothers and teachers
and shopkeepers, build it of strangers,
some of them family. Build it of sky
in unfamiliar places.

Build it of faces, clouded
and fading from photos, from memory's
unbolted storeroom. Build it
of all the words left too late to be spoken,
lodged like thorns in your throat.
Build it of quietness, chinks of it spreading
like light from the edge of a shuttered window.

Build it of knowing that those days
are over. Build it of those days. Build it of these.
Build it of soldiers and shipping containers
and hard hats and high-vis vests.
Build it of trying to buy
the other kind of black dress.

Build it of trees, build it of weeds.
Build it of flowers sprouting from traffic cones.
Build it of voices embalmed on an answerphone,
thinking you hear them laugh
when you're on your own, missing the punchline.
Build it of madness and raving
and hurling your howl to the wind.

Build it of books with inscriptions that catch you
off-guard one night, late, browsing the shelves.
Build it of paper. Build it of paperwork. Build it of forms.
Build it of notices. Build it of random
diversions, phrases from surveys and polls
with boxes to tick, *sometimes* or *yes*.

Build it of failing hearts, build it of false starts,
build it of age and the dying of light.
Build it of rattling bars, build it of pubs
spilling their fear out onto the footpath,
build it of last drinks, build it of last toasts and last posts
and last rites, build it of last words, build it of lasting,
build it of finally sleeping the night.

Build it of gestures, futile and otherwise.
Build it of faces in rear-view mirrors,
build it of hands outstretched in the darkness, hands
falling to fists, gripping the phone, the frame of a door.
Build it of words, filling with smoke and concrete dust.
Build it of all the things still to be done.

Build it for all we have lost,
for all our losses to come.

iii.

Fare

Oh what can ail thee knight-at-arms
Alone and palely loitering?

– JOHN KEATS

A bitter cold night with scudding rain,
a night for slinking cats, and taxi drivers
mopping up the stragglers spilled from pubs
      and nightclub doorways.

I was fiddling with the heater when she
slipped into my cab. Her arms were bare
and smooth and very pale. Her hair was red
      and garlanded

with pearls of rain, though her face and dress were dry.
I cleared my throat. Where to? – *Anywhere.* She caught
my startled glance in the rear-view mirror
      and held it there,

a grave smile playing across her lips. *Just*
drive around, for now. We've got all night
and I have time to kill, she said, and *Please.*
      And so I did.

She was lovely – I don't have the words
to conjure up her likeness. She seemed young,
but there was something in her eyes that spoke
      of lifetimes gone.

Around her face her hair hung like a prophecy,
long and red and rich – a man might give
his soul and think it cheap to know such wealth
     flow through his hands.

Drive, she said, and settled back in shadow.
There was something cat-like in the grace
of her repose. Beside her door, the streetlight
     flickered out.

I drove her through a city drowned in sleep.
Streets named for fallen saints dissolved to rivers
in the rain, and flowed south between
     the solemness of trees.

I heard her soft, contented sigh. I drove
until the rhythm of the tyres against
wet tar became a song, and the cab
     a throat to sing it.

I drove until the meter lost its tongue
and everywhere the traffic lights were turned
to whirling fireflies. I heard her laugh,
     and clap her hands,

and even in the mirror I could see
her wild, wild eyes. Something had changed, and I
was suddenly afraid – the strung bow of the hunter
     in her smile.

Now, she said, *it's time.* Her voice was gentle
and so soft I half expected that her
lips would brush my ear, her breath my cheek. *Back
     to the city.*

We drove, and the streets began to empty
into darkness, department stores deserted
but for mannequins in last month's clothes, and moths
    with pauper's wings.

I've known this city all my life – each bridge,
each cul-de-sac, each block – but now,
as though she'd summoned them, new streets appeared
    and we drove on

turning left, always *left, against the clock*
into a city changed, and changing, in
to neighbourhoods that never were before.
    Streetlights wavered

·through windscreen's brimming lens of water,
through the wipers' keening gesture. In the
sullen rain the buildings hunched their shoulders
    and lay down.

I saw the church where I was married pulled
apart, its bricks and stone stacked onto pallets,
its spire a child's toy, tumbled on the grass.
    Another corner,

and against the sky a stairwell reached out
past its shattered building into space –
I tried to speak, to ask, to plead, but the words
    twisted and set.

I drove through a broken city, and I wept.
Her fingers touched my face, and they were cold.
I heard her take each salt tear to her tongue
    and swallow them.

We passed beneath the steel and concrete belly
of a bridge into an empty lot, a dead end,
so I killed the lights, and turned
        the engine off.

I listened to the plinking as it cooled,
the rain in fretful handfuls on the roof.
I heard her sigh, drew a ragged breath
        and closed my eyes

and felt the small hairs lifting on my neck.
'What is this place?' I barely recognised the voice
to be my own, but I heard the smile in hers:
        This? Almost home.

Come with me. There's nothing for you back there
anymore. In the mirror I could see
her lean towards me, see the hunger in
        her eyes, and I

was lost, I was drowning in the well
of her will, the waters closing over me,
drunk as bees in autumn on the perfume
        of her skin.

Come with me. I couldn't have refused her
any more than unfurl wings and dash myself
against her, like a moth. *Come with me.*
        I reached blindly

for the door, jerked the handle, but it stuck
or it was locked, and as I swung around
to face her for the first time, I was dazzled
        by the headlights

of a car that flashed into existence in a heartbeat
in a street I knew, with buildings standing
whole in silhouette against the sky,
         and she was gone,

as if she'd never been. I heard the meter
click, and sat there, barely breathing, just
listening to the small sounds of a city
         deep in dreaming.

The night was old; a threadbare coat, too worn
to offer comfort. I stared at darkness,
watched it gather in the mirror's empty eye,
         But then I saw.

A passing headlight swung across the cab
and picked it out in flame – an ember etched
into the very fabric of the air,
         and then I knew

that it had all been true – a long, red hair.
Helpless, I watched it drift and fall and settle,
a tendril that burned into my skin
         – dear god, it burned.

It binds me to her still.

Burning

Late afternoon, and I'm burning tree-stumps. This one, deep in the cattle-camp of scribbly gums, sticking out a metre, with a sharp point like the one that bled the broodmare dry. I build the twig-pile around the base, burn the wood-witch at the stake. Bullgrass and bark-pith tucked under. The match flares like a curse, like a hole ripped open into another world. Friend and enemy, servant perpetually on the point of rebellion. Blessings laid at the foot of the mountain. I lean close, give it my breath.

                                                            sunset
                    the last glimmer
                    goes out

Matadora

Did you think I would run?

I can see strength
without weakening.

You are only hide and bone,
after all. A frame

to embroider with symbols
and emblems – a small death

to conquer again.

I will garland your neck
with ribbons of blood.

Fetish, kneel at my feet.
You are vessel, you are chair

for me to straddle, yes
you are drum.

Now *come*.

Seamstress

Last, she packed up her sewing machine
and the bright spools of thread,
the kaleidoscope of bobbins
that he'd reorganised by colour
and emotional connotation.

She'd already dismantled
the headless, limbless dummy,
with its expandable bosom
and retractable waist
that he'd found so alluring.

In the hall on the way out
she tweaked each
of the paintings askew,
bestowed a lipsticked kiss
on his mother's photograph,

and drove away surrounded by boxes,
tooting her horn to the neighbours
and smiling at the rear-view mirror;
him in the doorway, arms full
of fly-less trousers.

In The House of Fallen Roses

The dogs of summer are roaming, restless,
looking for someone like me
to tickle their bellies.
           They'll slink back home
in time for dawn and their
honey-scented wives.

In this house, we are all nectar,
scopa and sepal, mistress
and pack, full-bellied moon
and howl. There are worse ways to live
than from red lace curtains
and summer strays, hearing them
whimper, making them beg.

           I lose where I am,
who he is.
       Pollen.
          Bark
rough against my legs, astride
the old farm gate, swinging back
and forth,
       gently now –
          gone down,
sun still pearling my skin.
The dog's tongue lapping salt
from the arch of my throat
when I bend to meet him, the taste
of sea spray,
       a cut meadow, open
and parched beneath summer stars.

The messenger

Not a red rose or a satin heart

                 – CAROL ANN DUFFY

Not a postcard, or a tease
of lace.
In my absence I send
a strange messenger, my love
but true –

I send a spoon.

Its haft slips into your hand
gladly, like mine,
returns the faint warmth
of fingers and thumb

helpful as a wife.

The curve of its bowl
against your lips –
know this
for the bow of mine.

Let it rest there
the winter moon's reflection
reaching across a lake,
across the night's dark throat.

It scents
everything you taste.

And at night
it will nestle in the drawer
and croon its song of longing

to the quiet house
to our half-empty bed.

Astonishment

It had been an astonishing night. Heavy still
with the perfumed languor of what, she was sure
from her reading, had been *passion*, and possibly
sin – but deliciously so, delectably so,
archingly, tinglingly, voluptuously so –
so it came as a shock to discover
her paramour no longer quite as he
had been. In fact – and in her bed – turned
to ash.

        The shape of him printed
in powdered relief on the sheets. The colour
of concrete cemetery statues, or coils
of barbed wire, or tarnished spoons.
She whispered his name, or the name
she thought he had claimed as his,
the dust of him dancing in answer.
She traced her forefinger through him, as though
signing something away. Brought just a pinch of him
to her tongue – chalky, a hint of smoke,
almost sweet.

        She kept her back
to him as she dressed, still bashful.
She scooped him into a Spode-ware bowl,
dipped a damp brush in the powder,
swept him through her hair, like the fine brume
that rises from ploughed fields at night.
She used him to shadow her eyes, and stared

in the mirror at somebody older,
surer, a woman to reckon with –

not like a tally-stick, notched and split,
nor like an abacus, a broker's rosary.
More like a lodestone and needle, a compass
to guide with, a sextant to plot a true course.
But still more like a city astir at night, lights blazing
from every door – and no traveller, crossing
the darkness could be certain if these
were beacons of welcome,
or a city preparing for war.

Lares and penates

God of the river, its laughing mouth,
god of secrets singing rain to the roof,
god of the paddocks, god of the track
leading safely through the boggy creek,
god of the lilly pilly, god of the silver net
strung between gateposts, catching the stars.

Every outcrop, every ridge, every stand
of trees – guardians of the border
woven between earth and sky –
so many threads, our stories, braided
and tasselled or tucked
neatly into the backing –
the mountain
with great-grandfather's name,
the three silky oaks, heeled-in overnight
that grew into one – god
of the spendthrift
Christmas beetles, their jewels
scattered underfoot by morning.

The sun on the far ridge, flooding my veins.
The shifting course of the river in spate,
swelling the tone of my voice.
How could you live, rootless, unclaimed?
How can you stand, so far
from the bones of the mountain?

How else, when the child disappeared –
paddocks and solemn cattle, snakes
and long grass waving, waving,
the ripples spread wider, the barn,
the car shed, the sullen pond,
the underworld beneath the house,
the boar with his mouth full of razors,
the hooved, the toothed, the tusked –
did they find me unharmed, a mile from home
asleep on the hillside,
the kelpie bitch standing guard at my head,
unless cradled and claimed by something
that knows us all?

Trespass

In the pool of light from the bedside lamp
your hands rest like shadows.
It's one in the morning,
and you've fallen asleep, reading.

Where are you, my love? Where
are you wandering, slipped off from the raft
of your book, and into dark waters?

From the vase on our chest of drawers
an autumn leaf falls, lands lightly
on the surface. The faint musk of it
comforts me. I watch it float and drift
as the ripples ebb away and away

and something unknowable
wades out onto the furthest shore.

Earthrise

To feel the always coming on
The always rising of the night

– ARCHIBALD MACLEISH

Tethered by a thought, as much
as by the slender umbilical
– half a metre for every year of her life –

she hangs in space above
the slow-turning planet,
tiny as a moth, orbiting

a streetlamp at the end
of a deserted road – houses
guarded by ranks of sullen weeds,

snowflakes drifting through
a broken gable, shards of glass
dulling in the sodden carpet.

And everywhere the mist –
a grey tide gathering
into a silent sea,

broken only by the stanchion,
its sallow sodium glow,
the moth's ragged circling,

and the astronaut, staring down
into the well
of cloud and weather,

the gold flash from her visor
as she bends
to take the earth's confession.

Clemency

September: the month of your birth.
This morning the curtains mumbled at me –
fat and sleepy, a bumblebee the size
of my thumb's first joint
had dossed down for the night in their folds.
It stumbled across the peaks
of my fingers.
Our parents are elderly, you wrote.
Whatever it was I did, they need
you and me to get past this.
Somewhere there's a photograph
you sent me long ago, of prayer flags, a glass-blue sky,
and the snowy scalp of Chomolungma.
Whenever I brush my hair, our mother's face
is behind the mirror.

In the garden this clement morning, the bees
were drunk in the rhododendrons,
rioting colour and scent, a hum dithering
at the fabric of the day, like the static
of background conversation
on a phone call from a busy café.
You sent me a photo of mountains
crowned with a shrine
and a military helicopter.
The refugee I found this morning
was large enough to be a queen –
a hood of fur around her face, dark
jewelled eyes reading the world
in a language I can't even see.

Did you know they've found
a bumblebee colony in the rocks
above Everest Base Camp?
Almost as high as you've been,
up where the air is so thin
snow and ice can't melt,
but only evaporate.

When I opened the window
to let the bee fly free, she clung
for a moment, tapping her feet
as though sending a message in Morse,
or the way a climber tests the ice
at the edge of an alpine crevasse.
Whatever it was I did ... tell me,
what holds between us
other than blood?
We were born in a land so old
the mountains
were worn down to their bones.
The mountain you long for
is young and fierce,
and claims fistfuls of climbers each year.

Outside my window, pollen is falling,
a gold dust across leaf and stem.
In your mountains, the window for climbing
is a handful of weeks at the end of spring.
The buzzing sound in your ears
is caused by altitude sickness.
I've written you up to the plateau,
Camp Four – the South Col.

It is midnight, and time to begin
the ascent.
Each spring a bumblebee queen
begins anew alone –
finds a nest for herself, raises the first
of her brood in a silent catacomb.
Climb. I will write your axe
biting, your gloved hands sure
on the ropes, the strain
on your arms and your lungs.
Soon the sun will rise
and trickle its honey across
the snow. *Climb*. There is
bad blood between us.
The buzzing you feel
is hypoxia: too little air.
You don't have much time.
Climb. I still don't know
if I will write you back to safety
or leave you there.

Nightfall

Little by little, day winds down
its props, its scaffold of light.
The sun is slipped into its case,

and a woman with a basket
of washing is the last pin
holding back the curtain of night,

the tumble and the weight of it.

Notes

'Female, nude' was written for Helen Lowe, and triggered (in part) by Man Ray's 'Le Violon d'Ingres.'

'Classical Gas' is an iconic piece of guitar music, composed and originally performed by American guitarist Mason Williams in 1968.

'Chronicle of the year 793' is set on Lindisfarne, off the northwest coast of England; 793 AD was the year of the first Viking raids and the sacking of the monastery.

'The elephant in the parlour' nods to the title poem from Michael Harlow's *Today is the Piano's Birthday* (Auckland University Press, 1981).

'Lijessenthoek' is the second largest of the cemeteries for Commonwealth soldiers who were killed in the Ypres Salient on the Western Front in World War I. It is maintained by the Belgian government.

'The disembodied woman' weaves together quotes attributed to Marilyn Monroe with details from the chapter 'The Disembodied Lady' in Oliver Sacks' *The Man Who Mistook His Wife for a Hat* (Picador, 1986).

'Criccieth' is the Anglicised name of the town on the southern side of the Llyn Peninsula (North Wales). As Welsh does not use a double c, the proper spelling would be 'Cricieth'.

'Wintering over' won the 2003 Yellow Moon Seed Pearls haibun competition.

'The salmon' borrows and modifies a number of phrases from Ted Hughes' 'October Salmon' from *River* (Faber & Faber, 1983). The poem was highly commended in the 2008 New Zealand Poetry Society competition.

'Margaret of Finchley' was better known as Maggie Thatcher. She was the MP for the borough of Finchley from 1959 to 1992.

'Galanthus in rain' is a decima: ten lines of ten(ish) syllables, sharing a common polysyllabic end rhyme. *Galanthus nivalis* is the scientific name of the common snowdrop.

'Fault' refers to the time that the second and most damaging earthquake hit Christchurch on 22 February 2011.

'The Ministry of Sorrow' was triggered by an article in the Christchurch *Press* by reporter Islay McLeod ('Be ready, citizens, for stark reality', published 5 October 2011). She'd been into the red zone and been shocked by the damage, and didn't know how to react. From the article:

> *Hugh Nicholson, principal adviser for urban design at the Christchurch City Council, observed that we have people dealing with parks and people dealing with sewers. 'Yet we don't deal with emotions or people's experiences very well ... We don't have a Department of Sorrow.'*

'Fare' translates John Keats' 'La Belle Dame Sans Merci' into modern-day Christchurch. It is dedicated to the memory of John O'Connor.

'The messenger' was inspired by a tradition in Welsh poetry of sending a distant lover an object – and an accompanying poem – to stand in your place until you can be reunited.

'Lares and penates' were the household gods of ancient Rome – deities who looked after a particular village, or a particular house, or even just a particular family.

'Earthrise' was selected for *Best New Zealand Poems* (2014).

Acknowledgements

My thanks to the editors of the publications where versions of these poems appeared: *Across the Fingerboards* (NZPS, 2010), *Before the Sirocco* (NZPS, 2008), *Best New Zealand Poems* (IIML, 2014), *Chronogram* (USA), *Contemporary Haibun Online* (USA), *Contemporary Haibun vol. 8* (Red Moon Press, 2007), *Dear Heart: 150 New Zealand love poems* (Random House, 2012), *Frogpond* (USA), *Island* (Aus), *JAAM*, *Landfall*, *Leaving the Red Zone: Poems from the Canterbury earthquakes* (Clerestory Press, 2016), *Magma* (UK), *Poetry New Zealand*, *Simply Haiku* (UK), *Spin, takahē, The Tuesday Poem*, and *Yellow Moon* (Aus).

Much gratitude to Lynn Austin, Bella Boyd, Jeni Curtis, Shirley Eng, Gail Ingram, Janet Wainscott, Helen Yong and Karen Zelas for helping me bring these poems to fruition. Many thanks to David Howard and James Norcliffe for their advice and support over many years, not to mention the provision of kicks to the backside when they thought I needed them.

But most of all, thanks to Stewart. Without you, none of this would ever be possible.

Published by Otago University Press
Te Whare Tā o Te Wānanga o Ōtākou
533 Castle Street
Dunedin, New Zealand
university.press@otago.ac.nz
www.otago.ac.nz/press

First published 2021

ISBN 978-1-99-004819-7

Editor: Lynley Edmeades
Cover art: Crispin Korschen

Printed in New Zealand by Ligare